THE
ORDER OF MASS

ST PAULS

Cover: Logo of the 50th International Eucharistic Congress 2012 with the theme, 'The Eucharist, Communion with Christ and with One Another'. Logo designed by Martin Barlow, reproduced with permission of IEC2012.

Cover design: Middledot, London

Concordat cum Originali: Jane Porter

Imprimatur: Most Rev. Peter Smith, Archbishop of Southwark, 18 July 2011.

ST PAULS Publishing
187 Battersea Bridge Road, London SW11 3AS, UK
www.stpaulspublishing.com

Copyright © ST PAULS UK, 2011

ISBN 978-0-85439-817-1

A catalogue record is available for this book from the British Library.

Set by Tukan DTP, Stubbington, Fareham, UK
Printed by Bishops Printers Limited, Portsmouth, UK

ST PAULS is an activity of the priests and brothers
of the Society of St Paul who proclaim the Gospel
through the media of social communication.

The Introductory Rites

The Introductory Rites help the faithful come together as one, establish communion and prepare themselves properly to listen to the Word of God and to celebrate the Eucharist worthily.

All stand.

Celebrant: In the name of the Father, and of the Son, and of the Holy Spirit.

All: **Amen**.

Greeting

C: The grace of our Lord Jesus Christ,
and the love of God,
and the communion of the Holy Spirit
be with you all.

Or:

Grace to you and peace from God our Father
and the Lord Jesus Christ.

Or:

The Lord be with you.

All: **And with your spirit**.

The Priest, or a Deacon, or another minister, may very briefly introduce the Mass of the day to the faithful.

Penitential Act

C: Brethren (brothers and sisters), let us acknowledge our sins, and so prepare ourselves to celebrate the sacred mysteries.

(A brief silence)

All: I confess to almighty God
and to you, my brothers and sisters,
that I have greatly sinned,
in my thoughts and in my words,
in what I have done and in what I have failed to do,

And, striking their breast, they say:

through my fault, through my fault,
through my most grievous fault;

therefore I ask blessed Mary ever-Virgin,
all the Angels and Saints,
and you, my brothers and sisters,
to pray for me to the Lord our God.

C: May almighty God have mercy on us,
forgive us our sins,
and bring us to everlasting life.

All: **Amen.**

Or:

C: Have mercy on us, O Lord.
All: **For we have sinned against you.**

C: Show us, O Lord, your mercy.
All: **And grant us your salvation.**

C: May almighty God have mercy on us,
forgive us our sins,
and bring us to everlasting life.

Or:

C: You were sent to heal the contrite of heart:
    Lord, have mercy.   Or: Kyrie, eleison.
All: **Lord, have mercy**.   Or: **Kyrie, eleison.**

4

C: You came to call sinners:
Christ, have mercy.   Or: Christe, eleison.
All: **Christ, have mercy**.   Or: **Christe, eleison**.

C: You are seated at the right hand of the Father
to intercede for us:
Lord, have mercy.   Or: Kyrie, eleison.
All: **Lord, have mercy**.   Or: **Kyrie, eleison**.

C: May almighty God have mercy on us,
forgive us our sins,
and bring us to everlasting life.

The Kyrie, eleison (Lord, have mercy) invocations may follow.

V. Lord, have mercy.   R. **Lord, have mercy.**
V. Christ, have mercy.   R. **Christ, have mercy.**
V. Lord, have mercy.   R. **Lord, have mercy.**

Or:

V. Kyrie, eleison.   R. **Kyrie, eleison.**
V. Christe, eleison.   R. **Christe, eleison.**
V. Kyrie, eleison.   R. **Kyrie, eleison.**

The Gloria

When indicated this hymn is either sung or said:

Glory to God in the highest,
and on earth peace to people of good will.
We praise you,
we bless you,
we adore you,
we glorify you,
we give you thanks for your great glory,

Lord God, heavenly King,
O God, almighty Father.

Lord Jesus Christ, Only Begotten Son,
Lord God, Lamb of God, Son of the Father,
you take away the sins of the world,
    have mercy on us;
you take away the sins of the world,
    receive our prayer;
you are seated at the right hand of the Father,
    have mercy on us.

For you alone are the Holy One,
you alone are the Lord,
you alone are the Most High,
Jesus Christ,
with the Holy Spirit,
in the glory of God the Father.
Amen.

Glo-ry to God in the high-est,

and on earth peace to peo-ple of good will.

We praise you, we bless you, we a-dore you, we glo-ri-fy you,

we give you thanks for your great glo-ry,

Lord God, heav-en-ly King, O God, al-might-y Fa-ther.

Lord Je-sus Christ, On-ly Be-got-ten Son,

Lord God, Lamb of God, Son of the Fa-ther,

you take a-way the sins of the world, have mer-cy on us;

you take a-way the sins of the world, re-ceive our prayer;

you are seat-ed at the right hand of the Fa-ther, have mer-cy on us.

For you a-lone are the Ho-ly One, you a-lone are the Lord,

you a-lone are the Most High, Je-sus Christ, with the Ho-ly Spir-it,

in the glo-ry of God the Fa - ther. A - men.

The Collect

C: Let us pray.

All pray in silence with the Priest for a while.

Then the Priest says the Collect prayer.

All: **Amen.**

The Liturgy of the Word

By hearing the word proclaimed in worship, the faithful again enter into the unending dialogue between God and the covenant people, a dialogue sealed in the sharing of the Eucharisitc food and drink. The proclamation of the word is thus integral to the Mass and at its very centre.

All sit.

First Reading

To indicate the end of these readings, the reader acclaims:

The word of the Lord.

All: **Thanks be to God.**

Psalm

After the First Reading the psalmist or cantor sings or says the Psalm, with the people making the response.

Second Reading

On Sundays and certain other days there is a second reading. It concludes with the same responsory as above.

Gospel

The assembly stands to sing the Gospel Acclamation.

At the ambo the Deacon, or the Priest, says:

The Lord be with you.

All: **And with your spirit.**

The Deacon, or the Priest:

A reading from the holy Gospel according to N.

He makes the Sign of the Cross on the book and, together with the people, on his forehead, lips, and breast.

At the same time the people acclaim:

Glory to you, O Lord.

At the end of the Gospel, the Deacon, or the Priest, acclaims:

The Gospel of the Lord.

All: **Praise to you, Lord Jesus Christ.**

After the proclamation of the Gospel the congregation is seated.

The Homily

At the end of the Homily it is appropriate for there to be a brief silence for recollection.

The congregation then stands.

The Creed

On Sundays and Solemnities, the Profession of Faith or Creed will follow.

The Niceno-Constantinopolitan Creed

I believe in one God,
the Father almighty,
maker of heaven and earth,
of all things visible and invisible.

I believe in one Lord Jesus Christ,
the Only Begotten Son of God,
born of the Father before all ages.
God from God, Light from Light,
true God from true God,
begotten, not made, consubstantial with the Father;
through him all things were made.
For us men and for our salvation
he came down from heaven,

At the words that follow, up to and including **and became man**, all bow.

9

and by the Holy Spirit was incarnate of the Virgin Mary,
and became man.
For our sake he was crucified under Pontius Pilate,
he suffered death and was buried,
and rose again on the third day
in accordance with the Scriptures.
He ascended into heaven
and is seated at the right hand of the Father.
He will come again in glory
to judge the living and the dead
and his kingdom will have no end.

I believe in the Holy Spirit, the Lord, the giver of life,
who proceeds from the Father and the Son,
who with the Father and the Son is adored and glorified,
who has spoken through the prophets.

I believe in one, holy, catholic and apostolic Church.
I confess one Baptism for the forgiveness of sins
and I look forward to the resurrection of the dead
and the life of the world to come. Amen.

The Apostles' Creed

I believe in God,
the Father almighty,
Creator of heaven and earth,
and in Jesus Christ, his only Son, our Lord,

At the words that follow, up to and including the Virgin Mary, all bow.

who was conceived by the Holy Spirit,
born of the Virgin Mary,
suffered under Pontius Pilate,
was crucified, died and was buried;

he descended into hell;
on the third day he rose again from the dead;
he ascended into heaven,
and is seated at the right hand of God the Father almighty;
from there he will come to judge the living and the dead.

I believe in the Holy Spirit,
the holy catholic Church,
the communion of saints,
the forgiveness of sins,
the resurrection of the body,
and life everlasting. Amen.

The Prayer of the Faithful (Bidding Prayers)

After each intention there is a pause while the faithful pray.
Each intention may be concluded with a responsory such as:

The minister: Lord, in your mercy
All: Hear our prayer.

The Priest concludes the Prayer with a collect.

The Liturgy of the Eucharist

For Catholics, the Eucharist is the source and summit of the whole Christian life. It is the vital centre of all that the Church is and does, because at its heart is the real presence of the crucified, risen and glorified Lord, continuing and making available his saving work among us.

The Preparation of the Gifts

Presentation of the gifts

C: Blessed are you, Lord God of all creation,
for through your goodness we have received
the bread we offer you:
fruit of the earth and work of human hands,
it will become for us the bread of life.

All: **Blessed be God for ever.**

C: Blessed are you, Lord God of all creation,
for through your goodness we have received
the wine we offer you:
fruit of the vine and work of human hands,
it will become our spiritual drink.

All: **Blessed be God for ever**.

Pray, brethren (brothers and sisters),
that my sacrifice and yours
may be acceptable to God,
the almighty Father.

All: **May the Lord accept the sacrifice at your hands
for the praise and glory of his name,
for our good and the good of all his holy Church**.

Amen.

THE EUCHARISTIC PRAYER

The Eucharistic Prayer, the centre and summit of the entire celebration is a memorial proclamation of praise and thanksgiving for God's work of salvation, a proclamation in which the Body and Blood of Christ are made present by the power of the Holy Spirit and the people are joined to Christ in offering his Sacrifice to the Father.

Dialogue of the Preface.

C: The Lord be with you.

All: **And with your spirit**.

C: Lift up your hearts.

All: **We lift them up to the Lord**.

C: Let us give thanks to the Lord our God.

All: **It is right and just**.

The Priest continues with the Preface.
(See selection of Prefaces in the Altar Missal.)

Holy, Holy, Holy Lord God of hosts.
Heaven and earth are full of your glory.
Hosanna in the highest.
Blessed is he who comes in the name of the Lord.
Hosanna in the highest.

After the singing of the Sanctus the congregation kneels for the remainder of the Eucharistic Prayer.

EUCHARISTIC PRAYER I
(THE ROMAN CANON)

The Priest alone recites:

To you, therefore, most merciful Father,
we make humble prayer and petition
through Jesus Christ, your Son, our Lord:
that you accept
and bless ✠ these gifts, these offerings,
these holy and unblemished sacrifices,
which we offer you firstly
for your holy catholic Church.
Be pleased to grant her peace,
to guard, unite and govern her
throughout the whole world,
together with your servant N. our Pope
and N. our Bishop,*
and all those who, holding to the truth,
hand on the catholic and apostolic faith.

Remember, Lord, your servants N. and N.
and all gathered here,
whose faith and devotion are known to you.
For them, we offer you this sacrifice of praise
or they offer it for themselves
and all who are dear to them:
for the redemption of their souls,
in hope of health and well-being,
and paying their homage to you,
the eternal God, living and true.

---

* Mention may be made here of the Coadjutor Bishop, or Auxiliary
Bishops.

In communion with those whose memory we venerate,
especially the glorious ever-Virgin Mary,
Mother of our God and Lord, Jesus Christ,
and blessed Joseph, her Spouse,
your blessed Apostles and Martyrs,
Peter and Paul, Andrew,
(James, John,
Thomas, James, Philip,
Bartholomew, Matthew,
Simon and Jude;
Linus, Cletus, Clement, Sixtus,
Cornelius, Cyprian,
Lawrence, Chrysogonus,
John and Paul,
Cosmas and Damian)
and all your Saints;
we ask that through their merits and prayers,
in all things we may be defended
by your protecting help.
(Through Christ our Lord. Amen.)

Therefore, Lord, we pray:
graciously accept this oblation of our service,
that of your whole family;
order our days in your peace,
and command that we be delivered from eternal damnation
and counted among the flock of those you have chosen.
(Through Christ our Lord. Amen.)

Be pleased, O God, we pray,
to bless, acknowledge,
and approve this offering in every respect;
make it spiritual and acceptable,

so that it may become for us
the Body and ✠ Blood of your most beloved Son,
our Lord Jesus Christ.

On the day before he was to suffer,
he took bread in his holy and venerable hands,
and with eyes raised to heaven
to you, O God, his almighty Father,
giving you thanks, he said the blessing,
broke the bread
and gave it to his disciples, saying:

TAKE THIS, ALL OF YOU, AND EAT OF IT,
FOR THIS IS MY BODY,
WHICH WILL BE GIVEN UP FOR YOU.

In a similar way, when supper was ended,
he took this precious chalice
in his holy and venerable hands,
and once more giving you thanks, he said the blessing
and gave the chalice to his disciples, saying:

TAKE THIS, ALL OF YOU, AND DRINK FROM IT,
FOR THIS IS THE CHALICE OF MY BLOOD,
THE BLOOD OF THE NEW AND ETERNAL COVENANT,
WHICH WILL BE POURED OUT FOR YOU AND FOR MANY
FOR THE FORGIVENESS OF SINS.
DO THIS IN MEMORY OF ME.

The mystery of faith.

The people continue, acclaiming:

**We proclaim your Death, O Lord,
and profess your Resurrection
until you come again.**

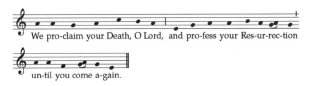

We pro-claim your Death, O Lord, and pro-fess your Res-ur-rec-tion un-til you come a-gain.

Or:

**When we eat this Bread and drink this Cup,
we proclaim your Death, O Lord,
until you come again.**

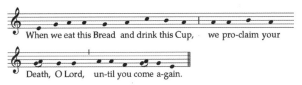

When we eat this Bread and drink this Cup, we pro-claim your Death, O Lord, un-til you come a-gain.

Or:

**Save us, Saviour of the world,
for by your Cross and Resurrection
you have set us free.**

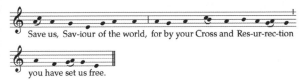

Save us, Sav-iour of the world, for by your Cross and Res-ur-rec-tion you have set us free.

Then the Priest alone continues:

Therefore, O Lord,
as we celebrate the memorial of the blessed Passion,
the Resurrection from the dead,

and the glorious Ascension into heaven
of Christ, your Son, our Lord,
we, your servants and your holy people,
offer to your glorious majesty
from the gifts that you have given us,
this pure victim,
this holy victim,
this spotless victim,
the holy Bread of eternal life
and the Chalice of everlasting salvation.

Be pleased to look upon these offerings
with a serene and kindly countenance,
and to accept them,
as once you were pleased to accept
the gifts of your servant Abel the just,
the sacrifice of Abraham, our father in faith,
and the offering of your high priest Melchizedek,
a holy sacrifice, a spotless victim.

In humble prayer we ask you, almighty God:
command that these gifts be borne
by the hands of your holy Angel
to your altar on high
in the sight of your divine majesty,
so that all of us, who through this participation at the altar
receive the most holy Body and Blood of your Son,
may be filled with every grace and heavenly blessing.

(Through Christ our Lord. Amen.)

Remember also, Lord, your servants N. and N.,
who have gone before us with the sign of faith
and rest in the sleep of peace.

Grant them, O Lord, we pray,
and all who sleep in Christ,
a place of refreshment, light and peace.
(Through Christ our Lord. Amen.)

To us, also, your servants, who, though sinners,
hope in your abundant mercies,
graciously grant some share
and fellowship with your holy Apostles and Martyrs:
with John the Baptist, Stephen,
Matthias, Barnabas,
(Ignatius, Alexander,
Marcellinus, Peter,
Felicity, Perpetua,
Agatha, Lucy,
Agnes, Cecilia, Anastasia)
and all your Saints;
admit us, we beseech you,
into their company,
not weighing our merits,
but granting us your pardon,
through Christ our Lord.
Through whom
you continue to make all these good things, O Lord;
you sanctify them, fill them with life,
bless them, and bestow them upon us.

The Priest takes the chalice and the paten with the host and, raising both, he alone says:

Through him, and with him, and in him,
O God, almighty Father,

in the unity of the Holy Spirit,
all glory and honour is yours,
for ever and ever.

The people acclaim:

Amen.

Through him, and with him, and in him, O God, almighty Father,

in the unity of the Ho-ly Spir-it, all glo-ry and hon-our is yours,

for ev - er and ev-er. R. A-men.

Then follows the Communion Rite, p.44.

EUCHARISTIC PRAYER II

This Eucharistic Prayer has its own Preface, but it may also be used
with other Prefaces, especially those that present an overall view of
the mystery of salvation, such as the Common Prefaces.

V.   The Lord be with you.
R.   **And with your spirit**.

V.   Lift up your hearts.
R.   **We lift them up to the Lord**.

V.   Let us give thanks to the Lord our God.
R.   **It is right and just**.

V. The Lord be with you.　　R. And with your spir-it.

V. Lift up your hearts.　　R. We lift them up to the Lord.

V. Let us give thanks to the Lord our God.　　R. It is right and just.

It is truly right and just, our duty and our salvation,
always and everywhere to give you thanks,

Father most holy,
through your beloved Son, Jesus Christ,
your Word through whom you made all things,
whom you sent as our Saviour and Redeemer,
incarnate by the Holy Spirit and born of the Virgin.

Fulfilling your will and gaining for you a holy people,
he stretched out his hands as he endured his Passion,
so as to break the bonds of death
and manifest the resurrection.

And so, with the Angels and all the Saints
we declare your glory,
as with one voice we acclaim:

Holy, Holy, Holy Lord God of hosts.
Heaven and earth are full of your glory.
Hosanna in the highest.
Blessed is he who comes in the name of the Lord.
Hosanna in the highest.

You are indeed Holy, O Lord,
the fount of all holiness.
Make holy, therefore, these gifts, we pray,
by sending down your Spirit upon them like the dewfall,
so that they may become for us
the Body and ✠ Blood of our Lord Jesus Christ.

At the time he was betrayed
and entered willingly into his Passion,
he took bread and, giving thanks, broke it,
and gave it to his disciples, saying:

TAKE THIS, ALL OF YOU, AND EAT OF IT,
FOR THIS IS MY BODY,
WHICH WILL BE GIVEN UP FOR YOU.

In a similar way, when supper was ended,
he took the chalice
and, once more giving thanks,
he gave it to his disciples, saying:

TAKE THIS, ALL OF YOU, AND DRINK FROM IT,
FOR THIS IS THE CHALICE OF MY BLOOD,
THE BLOOD OF THE NEW AND ETERNAL COVENANT,
WHICH WILL BE POURED OUT FOR YOU AND FOR MANY
FOR THE FORGIVENESS OF SINS.
DO THIS IN MEMORY OF ME.

The mystery of faith.

The people continue, acclaiming:

**We proclaim your Death, O Lord,
and profess your Resurrection
until you come again.**

Or:

**When we eat this Bread and drink this Cup,
we proclaim your Death, O Lord,
until you come again.**

Or:

**Save us, Saviour of the world,
for by your Cross and Resurrection
you have set us free**.

Then the Priest alone continues:

Therefore, as we celebrate
the memorial of his Death and Resurrection,
we offer you, Lord,
the Bread of life and the Chalice of salvation,
giving thanks that you have held us worthy
to be in your presence and minister to you.

Humbly we pray
that, partaking of the Body and Blood of Christ,
we may be gathered into one by the Holy Spirit.

Remember, Lord, your Church,
spread throughout the world,
and bring her to the fullness of charity,
together with N. our Pope and N. our Bishop*
and all the clergy.

In Masses for the Dead, the following may be added:

Remember your servant N.,
whom you have called (today)
from this world to yourself.

---

* Mention may be made here of the Coadjutor Bishop, or Auxiliary
Bishops.

Grant that he (she) who was united with your Son
    in a death like his,
may also be one with him in his Resurrection.

Remember also our brothers and sisters
who have fallen asleep in the hope of the resurrection,
and all who have died in your mercy:
welcome them into the light of your face.

Have mercy on us all, we pray,
that with the Blessed Virgin Mary, Mother of God,
with the blessed Apostles,
and all the Saints who have pleased you throughout
    the ages,
we may merit to be coheirs to eternal life,
and may praise and glorify you
through your Son, Jesus Christ.

The Priest takes the chalice and the paten with the host and, raising both, he alone says:

Through him, and with him, and in him,
O God, almighty Father,
in the unity of the Holy Spirit,
all glory and honour is yours,
for ever and ever.

The people acclaim:

Amen.

Then follows the Communion Rite, p.44.

EUCHARISTIC PRAYER III

The Priest alone says:

You are indeed Holy, O Lord,
and all you have created
rightly gives you praise,
for through your Son our Lord Jesus Christ,
by the power and working of the Holy Spirit,
you give life to all things and make them holy,
and you never cease to gather a people to yourself,
so that from the rising of the sun to its setting
a pure sacrifice may be offered to your name.
Therefore, O Lord, we humbly implore you:
by the same Spirit graciously make holy
these gifts we have brought to you for consecration,
that they may become the Body and ✠ Blood
of your Son our Lord Jesus Christ,
at whose command we celebrate these mysteries.

For on the night he was betrayed
he himself took bread,
and, giving you thanks, he said the blessing,
broke the bread and gave it to his disciples, saying:

TAKE THIS, ALL OF YOU, AND EAT OF IT,
FOR THIS IS MY BODY,
WHICH WILL BE GIVEN UP FOR YOU.

In a similar way, when supper was ended,
he took the chalice,
and, giving you thanks, he said the blessing,
and gave the chalice to his disciples, saying:

TAKE THIS, ALL OF YOU, AND DRINK FROM IT,
FOR THIS IS THE CHALICE OF MY BLOOD,

THE BLOOD OF THE NEW AND ETERNAL COVENANT,
WHICH WILL BE POURED OUT FOR YOU AND FOR MANY
FOR THE FORGIVENESS OF SINS.
DO THIS IN MEMORY OF ME.

The mystery of faith.

The people continue, acclaiming:

**We proclaim your Death, O Lord,
and profess your Resurrection
until you come again.**

Or:

**When we eat this Bread and drink this Cup,
we proclaim your Death, O Lord,
until you come again.**

Or:

**Save us, Saviour of the world,
for by your Cross and Resurrection
you have set us free.**

The Priest alone continues:

Therefore, O Lord, as we celebrate the memorial
of the saving Passion of your Son,
his wondrous Resurrection
and Ascension into heaven,
and as we look forward to his second coming,
we offer you in thanksgiving
this holy and living sacrifice.

Look, we pray, upon the oblation of your Church
and, recognising the sacrificial Victim by whose death
you willed to reconcile us to yourself,

grant that we, who are nourished
by the Body and Blood of your Son
and filled with his Holy Spirit,
may become one body, one spirit in Christ.

May he make of us
an eternal offering to you,
so that we may obtain an inheritance with your elect,
especially with the most Blessed Virgin Mary,
    Mother of God,
with your blessed Apostles and glorious Martyrs,
(with Saint N.: the Saint of the day or Patron Saint)
and with all the Saints,
on whose constant intercession in your presence
we rely for unfailing help.

May this Sacrifice of our reconciliation,
we pray, O Lord,
advance the peace and salvation of all the world.
Be pleased to confirm in faith and charity
your pilgrim Church on earth,
with your servant N. our Pope and N. our Bishop,*
the Order of Bishops, all the clergy,
and the entire people you have gained for your own.

Listen graciously to the prayers of this family,
whom you have summoned before you:
in your compassion, O merciful Father,
gather to yourself all your children
scattered throughout the world.

---

*   Mention may be made here of the Coadjutor Bishop, or Auxiliary
   Bishops.

† To our departed brothers and sisters
and to all who were pleasing to you
at their passing from this life,
give kind admittance to your kingdom.

There we hope to enjoy for ever the fullness of your glory
through Christ our Lord,
through whom you bestow on the world all that is good.†

When this Eucharistic Prayer is used in Masses for the Dead, the
following may be said:

† Remember your servant N.
whom you have called (today)
from this world to yourself.
Grant that he (she) who was united with your Son
   in a death like his,
may also be one with him in his Resurrection,
when from the earth
he will raise up in the flesh those who have died,
and transform our lowly body
after the pattern of his own glorious body.
To our departed brothers and sisters, too,
and to all who were pleasing to you
at their passing from this life,
give kind admittance to your kingdom.
There we hope to enjoy for ever the fullness of your glory,
when you will wipe away every tear from our eyes.
For seeing you, our God, as you are,
we shall be like you for all the ages
and praise you without end,

He joins his hands.

through Christ our Lord,
through whom you bestow on the world all that is good.†

The Priest takes the chalice and the paten with the host and, raising both, he alone says:

Through him, and with him, and in him,
O God, almighty Father,
in the unity of the Holy Spirit,
all glory and honour is yours, for ever and ever.

The people acclaim:

Amen.

EUCHARISTIC PRAYER IV

It is not permitted to change the Preface of this Eucharistic Prayer because of the structure of the Prayer itself, which presents a summary of the history of salvation.

V.   The Lord be with you.
R.   **And with your spirit**.
V.   Lift up your hearts.
R.   **We lift them up to the Lord**.
V.   Let us give thanks to the Lord our God.
R.   **It is right and just**.

It is truly right to give you thanks,
truly just to give you glory, Father most holy,
for you are the one God living and true,
existing before all ages and abiding for all eternity,
dwelling in unapproachable light;
yet you, who alone are good, the source of life,
have made all that is,
so that you might fill your creatures with blessings
and bring joy to many of them by the glory of your light.

And so, in your presence are countless hosts of Angels,
who serve you day and night
and, gazing upon the glory of your face,
glorify you without ceasing.

With them we, too, confess your name in exultation,
giving voice to every creature under heaven,
as we acclaim:

Holy, Holy, Holy Lord God of hosts.
Heaven and earth are full of your glory.
Hosanna in the highest.
Blessed is he who comes in the name of the Lord.
Hosanna in the highest.

The Priest alone says:

We give you praise, Father most holy,
for you are great
and you have fashioned all your works
in wisdom and in love.
You formed man in your own image
and entrusted the whole world to his care,
so that in serving you alone, the Creator,
he might have dominion over all creatures.
And when through disobedience he had lost your friendship,
you did not abandon him to the domain of death.
For you came in mercy to the aid of all,
so that those who seek might find you.
Time and again you offered them covenants
and through the prophets
taught them to look forward to salvation.

And you so loved the world, Father most holy,
that in the fullness of time
you sent your Only Begotten Son to be our Saviour.
Made incarnate by the Holy Spirit
and born of the Virgin Mary,
he shared our human nature
in all things but sin.
To the poor he proclaimed the good news of salvation,

to prisoners, freedom,
and to the sorrowful of heart, joy.
To accomplish your plan,
he gave himself up to death,
and, rising from the dead,
he destroyed death and restored life.

And that we might live no longer for ourselves
but for him who died and rose again for us,
he sent the Holy Spirit from you, Father,
as the first fruits for those who believe,
so that, bringing to perfection his work in the world,
he might sanctify creation to the full.

Therefore, O Lord, we pray:
may this same Holy Spirit
graciously sanctify these offerings,
that they may become
the Body and ✠ Blood of our Lord Jesus Christ
for the celebration of this great mystery,
which he himself left us
as an eternal covenant.
For when the hour had come
for him to be glorified by you, Father most holy,
having loved his own who were in the world,
he loved them to the end:
and while they were at supper,
he took bread, blessed and broke it,
and gave it to his disciples, saying:

TAKE THIS, ALL OF YOU, AND EAT OF IT,
FOR THIS IS MY BODY,
WHICH WILL BE GIVEN UP FOR YOU.

In a similar way,
taking the chalice filled with the fruit of the vine,
he gave thanks,
and gave the chalice to his disciples, saying:

Take this, all of you, and drink from it,
for this is the chalice of my Blood,
the Blood of the new and eternal covenant,
which will be poured out for you and for many
for the forgiveness of sins.
Do this in memory of me.

The mystery of faith.

The people continue, acclaiming:

**We proclaim your Death, O Lord,
and profess your Resurrection
until you come again.**

Or:

**When we eat this Bread and drink this Cup,
we proclaim your Death, O Lord,
until you come again.**

Or:

**Save us, Saviour of the world,
for by your Cross and Resurrection
you have set us free.**

The Priest alone says:

Therefore, O Lord,
as we now celebrate the memorial of our redemption,
we remember Christ's Death
and his descent to the realm of the dead,
we proclaim his Resurrection

and his Ascension to your right hand,
and, as we await his coming in glory,
we offer you his Body and Blood,
the sacrifice acceptable to you
which brings salvation to the whole world.

Look, O Lord, upon the Sacrifice
which you yourself have provided for your Church,
and grant in your loving kindness
to all who partake of this one Bread and one Chalice
that, gathered into one body by the Holy Spirit,
they may truly become a living sacrifice in Christ
to the praise of your glory.

Therefore, Lord, remember now
all for whom we offer this sacrifice:
especially your servant N. our Pope,
N. our Bishop,* and the whole Order of Bishops,
all the clergy,
those who take part in this offering,
those gathered here before you,
your entire people,
and all who seek you with a sincere heart.

Remember also
those who have died in the peace of your Christ
and all the dead,
whose faith you alone have known.

---

* Mention may be made here of the Coadjutor Bishop, or Auxiliary
   Bishops.

To all of us, your children,
grant, O merciful Father,
that we may enter into a heavenly inheritance
with the Blessed Virgin Mary, Mother of God,
and with your Apostles and Saints in your kingdom.
There, with the whole of creation,
freed from the corruption of sin and death,
may we glorify you through Christ our Lord,
through whom you bestow on the world all that is good.

At the conclusion of the prayer the Priest takes the chalice and the paten with the host and, raising both, he alone says:

Through him, and with him, and in him,
O God, almighty Father,
in the unity of the Holy Spirit,
all glory and honour is yours,
for ever and ever.

The people acclaim:

Amen.

EUCHARISTIC PRAYER
FOR RECONCILIATION I

V. The Lord be with you.
R. **And with your spirit**.

V. Lift up your hearts.
R. **We lift them up to the Lord**.

V. Let us give thanks to the Lord our God.
R. **It is right and just**.

It is truly right and just
that we should always give you thanks,
Lord, holy Father, almighty and eternal God.

For you do not cease to spur us on
to possess a more abundant life
and, being rich in mercy,
you constantly offer pardon
and call on sinners
to trust in your forgiveness alone.

Never did you turn away from us,
and, though time and again we have broken your covenant,
you have bound the human family to yourself
through Jesus your Son, our Redeemer,
with a new bond of love so tight
that it can never be undone.

Even now you set before your people
a time of grace and reconciliation,
and, as they turn back to you in spirit,
you grant them hope in Christ Jesus
and a desire to be of service to all,
while they entrust themselves
more fully to the Holy Spirit.

And so, filled with wonder,
we extol the power of your love,
and, proclaiming our joy
at the salvation that comes from you,
we join in the heavenly hymn of countless hosts,
as without end we acclaim:

Holy, Holy, Holy Lord God of hosts.
Heaven and earth are full of your glory.
Hosanna in the highest.
Blessed is he who comes in the name of the Lord.
Hosanna in the highest.

The Priest, with hands extended, says:

You are indeed Holy, O Lord,
and from the world's beginning
are ceaselessly at work,
so that the human race may become holy,
just as you yourself are holy.

He joins his hands and, holding them extended over the offerings, says:

Look, we pray, upon your people's offerings
and pour out on them the power of your Spirit,

He joins his hands and makes the Sign of the Cross once over the bread and chalice together, saying:

that they may become the Body and ✠ Blood

He joins his hands.

of your beloved Son, Jesus Christ,
in whom we, too, are your sons and daughters.

Indeed, though we once were lost
and could not approach you,
you loved us with the greatest love:
for your Son, who alone is just,
handed himself over to death,
and did not disdain to be nailed for our sake
to the wood of the Cross.
But before his arms were outstretched
    between heaven and earth,
to become the lasting sign of your covenant,
he desired to celebrate the Passover with his disciples.

As he ate with them,
he took bread

and, giving you thanks, he said the blessing,
broke the bread and gave it to them, saying:

Take this, all of you, and eat of it,
for this is my Body,
which will be given up for you.

In a similar way, when supper was ended,
knowing that he was about to reconcile all things in himself
through his Blood to be shed on the Cross,
he took the chalice, filled with the fruit of the vine,
and once more giving you thanks,
handed the chalice to his disciples, saying:

Take this, all of you, and drink from it,
for this is the chalice of my Blood,
the Blood of the new and eternal covenant,
which will be poured out for you and for many
for the forgiveness of sins.
Do this in memory of me.

The mystery of faith.

**We proclaim your Death, O Lord,
and profess your Resurrection
until you come again**.

Or:

**When we eat this Bread and drink this Cup,
we proclaim your Death, O Lord,
until you come again.**

Or:

**Save us, Saviour of the world,
for by your Cross and Resurrection
you have set us free.**

Therefore, as we celebrate
the memorial of your Son Jesus Christ,
who is our Passover and our surest peace,
we celebrate his Death and Resurrection from the dead,
and looking forward to his blessed Coming,
we offer you, who are our faithful and merciful God,
this sacrificial Victim
who reconciles to you the human race.

Look kindly, most compassionate Father,
on those you unite to yourself
by the Sacrifice of your Son,
and grant that, by the power of the Holy Spirit,
as they partake of this one Bread and one Chalice,
they may be gathered into one Body in Christ,
who heals every division.

Be pleased to keep us always
in communion of mind and heart,
together with N. our Pope and N. our Bishop.*
Help us to work together
for the coming of your Kingdom,
until the hour when we stand before you,
Saints among the Saints in the halls of heaven,
with the Blessed Virgin Mary, Mother of God,
the blessed Apostles and all the Saints,
and with our deceased brothers and sisters,
whom we humbly commend to your mercy.

---

* Mention may be made here of the Coadjutor Bishop, or Auxiliary
Bishops.

Then, freed at last from the wound of corruption
and made fully into a new creation,
we shall sing to you with gladness
the thanksgiving of Christ,
who lives for all eternity.

He takes the chalice and the paten with the host and, raising both,
he says:

Through him, and with him, and in him,
O God, almighty Father,
in the unity of the Holy Spirit,
all glory and honour is yours,
for ever and ever.

The people acclaim:

Amen.

EUCHARISTIC PRAYER
FOR RECONCILIATION II

V.   The Lord be with you.
R.   **And with your spirit**.

V.   Lift up your hearts.
R.   **We lift them up to the Lord**.

V.   Let us give thanks to the Lord our God.
R.   **It is right and just**.

It is truly right and just
that we should give you thanks and praise,
O God, almighty Father,
for all you do in this world,
through our Lord Jesus Christ.

For though the human race
is divided by dissension and discord,
yet we know that by testing us
you change our hearts
to prepare them for reconciliation.

Even more, by your Spirit you move human hearts
that enemies may speak to each other again,
adversaries may join hands,
and peoples seek to meet together.

By the working of your power
it comes about, O Lord,
that hatred is overcome by love,
revenge gives way to forgiveness,
and discord is changed to mutual respect.

Therefore, as we give you ceaseless thanks
with the choirs of heaven,
we cry out to your majesty on earth,
and without end we acclaim:

Holy, Holy, Holy Lord God of hosts.
Heaven and earth are full of your glory.
Hosanna in the highest.
Blessed is he who comes in the name of the Lord.
Hosanna in the highest.

The Priest alone says:

You, therefore, almighty Father,
we bless through Jesus Christ your Son,
who comes in your name.

He himself is the Word that brings salvation,
the hand you extend to sinners,
the way by which your peace is offered to us.
When we ourselves had turned away from you
on account of our sins,
you brought us back to be reconciled, O Lord,
so that, converted at last to you,
we might love one another
through your Son,
whom for our sake you handed over to death.

And now, celebrating the reconciliation
Christ has brought us,
we entreat you:
sanctify these gifts by the outpouring of your Spirit,
that they may become the Body and ✠ Blood of your Son,
whose command we fulfil
when we celebrate these mysteries.

For when about to give his life to set us free,
as he reclined at supper,
he himself took bread into his hands,
and, giving you thanks, he said the blessing,
broke the bread and gave it to his disciples, saying:

TAKE THIS, ALL OF YOU, AND EAT OF IT,
FOR THIS IS MY BODY,
WHICH WILL BE GIVEN UP FOR YOU.

In a similar way, on that same evening,
he took the chalice of blessing in his hands,
confessing your mercy,
and gave the chalice to his disciples, saying:

Take this, all of you, and drink from it,
for this is the chalice of my Blood,
the Blood of the new and eternal covenant,
which will be poured out for you and for many
for the forgiveness of sins.
Do this in memory of me.

The mystery of faith.

And the people continue, acclaiming:

**We proclaim your Death, O Lord,
and profess your Resurrection
until you come again**.

Or:

**When we eat this Bread and drink this Cup,
we proclaim your Death, O Lord,
until you come again**.

Or:

**Save us, Saviour of the world,
for by your Cross and Resurrection
you have set us free**.

The Priest alone says:

Celebrating, therefore, the memorial
of the Death and Resurrection of your Son,
who left us this pledge of his love,
we offer you what you have bestowed on us,
the Sacrifice of perfect reconciliation.

Holy Father, we humbly beseech you
to accept us also, together with your Son,
and in this saving banquet
graciously to endow us with his very Spirit,
who takes away everything
that estranges us from one another.

May he make your Church a sign of unity
and an instrument of your peace among all people
and may he keep us in communion
with N. our Pope and N. our Bishop*
and all the Bishops
and your entire people.

Just as you have gathered us now at the table of your Son,
so also bring us together,
with the glorious Virgin Mary, Mother of God,
with your blessed Apostles and all the Saints,
with our brothers and sisters
and those of every race and tongue
who have died in your friendship.
Bring us to share with them the unending banquet of unity
in a new heaven and a new earth,
where the fullness of your peace will shine forth
in Christ Jesus our Lord.

The Priest takes the chalice and the paten with the host and, raising both, he alone says:

Through him, and with him, and in him,
O God, almighty Father,
in the unity of the Holy Spirit,
all glory and honour is yours,
for ever and ever.

The people continue:

Amen.

The Communion Rite

The eating and drinking together of the Lord's Body and Blood in a Paschal meal is the culmination of the Eucharist. The themes underlying these rites are the mutual love and reconciliation that are both the condition and the fruit of worthy communion and the unity of the many in the One.

The Lord's Prayer

The congregation stands and the Priest says:

At the Saviour's command
and formed by divine teaching,
we dare to say:

Together with the people, he continues:

**Our Father, who art in heaven,
hallowed be thy name;
thy kingdom come,
thy will be done
on earth as it is in heaven.
Give us this day our daily bread,
and forgive us our trespasses,
as we forgive those who trespass against us;
and lead us not into temptation,
but deliver us from evil.**

The Priest alone continues, saying:

Deliver us, Lord, we pray, from every evil,
graciously grant peace in our days,
that, by the help of your mercy,
we may be always free from sin
and safe from all distress,
as we await the blessed hope
and the coming of our Saviour, Jesus Christ.

The people conclude the prayer, acclaiming:

**For the kingdom,
the power and the glory are yours
now and for ever.**

Then the Priest alone says aloud:

Lord Jesus Christ,
who said to your Apostles:
Peace I leave you, my peace I give you,
look not on our sins,
but on the faith of your Church,
and graciously grant her peace and unity
in accordance with your will.
Who live and reign for ever and ever.

The people reply:

Amen.

C: The peace of the Lord be with you always.
All: **And with your spirit.**

The Deacon, or the Priest, adds:

Let us offer each other the sign of peace.

And all offer one another the customary sign of peace.

Breaking of the Bread

During the breaking of the host the following is sung or said:

**Lamb of God, you take away the sins of the world,
    have mercy on us.
Lamb of God, you take away the sins of the world,
    have mercy on us.
Lamb of God, you take away the sins of the world,
    grant us peace.**

Lamb of God, * you take a-way the sins of the world,

have mer-cy on us.

Lamb of God, * you take a-way the sins of the world,

have mer-cy on us.

Lamb of God, * you take a-way the sins of the world,

grant us peace.

After the Lamb of God, the people kneel.

Invitation to Communion

The Priest genuflects, takes the host and, holding it slightly raised above the paten or above the chalice says aloud:

Behold the Lamb of God,
behold him who takes away the sins of the world.
Blessed are those called to the supper of the Lamb.

All: **Lord, I am not worthy**
that you should enter under my roof,
but only say the word
and my soul shall be healed.

People come forward in reverent procession, and make a preparatory act of reverence by bowing their head in honour of Christ's presence in the sacrament. They receive Holy Communion standing.

The Priest says:

The Body (Blood) of Christ.

The communicant replies: **Amen** and receives communion.

A sacred silence or a psalm or other canticle of praise or a hymn may be sung.

Then, the Priest says:

Let us pray.

All stand and pray in silence. Then the Priest says the Prayer after Communion, at the end of which the people acclaim:

Amen.

The Concluding Rites

The brief Concluding Rite sends the people forth to put into effect in their daily lives the Mystery of Christ's Death and Resurrection and the unity in Christ which they have celebrated. Their mission is to witness to Christ in the world and to bring the Gospel to the poor.

C: The Lord be with you.
All: **And with your spirit.**

C: May almighty God bless you,
the Father, and the Son, ✠ and the Holy Spirit.
All: **Amen.**

Then the Deacon, or the Priest himself says:

Go forth, the Mass is ended.

> Or:

Go and announce the Gospel of the Lord.

> Or:

Go in peace, glorifying the Lord by your life.

> Or:

Go in peace.

The people reply:

Thanks be to God.